The Star That Changed a Young Boy's Life

by

Maria Angela Quiñones

Illustrations by Melanie Quiñones

Published by:

McDougal & Associates
www.thepublishedword.com

ISBN 978-1-964665-02-3

Printed on demand in the U.S.,
the U.K., Australia and the UAE
For Distribution Worldwide

Dedication

To my beloved sister, Luz Esther Rodriguez, whose life was a testament to the power of God's love and grace. God gave Esther the strength to battle daily for her life and the courage to face death, holding onto His promises—that His peace would be with her now and for eternity and that He would care for her two precious children, Joelle and Daniel. Esther faithfully served her church as a volunteer, teaching the children's Sunday School class, and imparted the love of God and His faithfulness to all. As a devoted school teacher, she inspired, not only her own children, but also the many she touched through her work and by her example. Her legacy of faith, love, and dedication continues to guide and inspire us all.

To my mom, Marina Quiñones, the wise woman of Proverbs, who taught us to love and fear God above everyone and everything else. Her remarkable persistence and perseverance in looking for God's face reached the heart of God. She blessed all her descendants with a legacy of faith and love.

To my dad, Hernando Quiñones, a musically gifted man of God. At a very early age, he discovered on his own his ability to play instruments. Dad used this gift as a worship leader and enjoyed teaching music to those who wanted to worship the Lord.

To my daughter, Maite Quiñones, who has been able to overcome the hard times of life by standing on the Rock of her salvation, Jesus Christ. God has given her a heart for the fatherless, and neglected children have found appreciation and respect in her classroom.

To my sister, Emma Paulina Quiñones, a strong woman of God, firmly rooted in Jesus Christ. She is a warrior in His kingdom, created to fight for His truth and glory. Her strength, faith, and unwavering commitment to God's will continue to inspire her two children, Rusbeh and Guiv, and us all.

To my brothers—Jorge, Hernando, Pablo, and Esteban—men of God who walk faithfully with the Lord Jesus.

Their hearts are set on Him alone, and their lives reflect His love, strength, and guidance. May they continue to be steadfast in their faith, shining as examples of His grace and truth to all who cross their paths.

Acknowledgments

This story would never have taken place were it not for the divine will of a loving God.

Thank you to godly grandparents who obediently listen to God's voice and walk the extra mile in the lives of their children and grandchildren to bring the love of God into their lives.

I thank the Holy Spirit for waking me up on a very cold Christmas morning and inspiring me to declare God's unconditional love for everyone who opens their heart to Him by telling the story of a broken family, a mother and her four children and the loving and godly grandparents God used to bring healing to their broken hearts, salvation to their souls, and hope for their future.

Yes, God uses parents, grandparents, or anyone who has a heart for the fatherless to bring His love to the brokenhearted. I pray that Jolene's story and our personal testimony will inspire you to be part of the healing process in the lives of those who do not know that God is the only one who makes orphans His own sons and daughters and fills them with His heavenly love.

Prologue

Thank you for accompanying me on this real-life story that happened on Christmas Eve.

The phone rang a few times before Grandma answered it. To her surprise, it was her baby girl, Jolene. She listened as devastating statements came from her precious princess's mouth. Grandma had to sit down to listen to the story. She did not interrupt, but her heart was broken, and tears streamed down her face. Internally, she was already praying, asking God to intervene in this situation. Her daughter and her four grandchildren had been abandoned by a man who did not understand the long-term consequences his selfish decision could have on them for the rest of their lives. What would happen to them now?

A few hours later, Grandma's house that had been so quiet now had lights shining everywhere, and four young boys were running up and down, hugging their grandparents and putting big smiles on their faces. This remarkable demonstration of love from a grandfather and his wife was God's love being extended to Jolene and her children.

Come, with me as we see what happened after Jolene and her four boys arrived at Grandma's home.

Introduction

The story you are about to read is true. It involves a family of four young boys and their mother abandoned by their father and forced to live with her parents on a small rural farm.

The mother had to work long hours to support her boys, and the boys who were old enough were required to do their part around the farm. The amazing thing is that rather than feel they were somehow suffering, being punished, or deprived of something, these boys looked upon farm life as great fun and also looked up to their grandparents with great respect. The result was a Christmas miracle that affected them all.

The story is told through the eyes of the oldest son, Dustin, for in the unfolding of it, he had a life-changing experience.

How do I know so much about this family and how they were impacted by a Christmas star? They were my dear neighbors and friends.

There was a reason that I became very emotionally involved in this situation. My dear neighbor and friend, Larry, came home one day devastated by the situation of his youngest daughter and her four small children. As he started to share with me their sad story, my mind went back to a time years before when I had gone through a similar painful situation.

My daughter Maite was only three when her father decided to leave us. We were thousands of miles away from my family, and with very limited economic resources, it was difficult for me to support myself, let alone a young daughter. I had some serious decisions to make.

If I continued to go to school and work at the same time, I would have to put Maite in an orphanage. I hated that thought. But the only other alternative I could think of was to ask my parents to open their home to both of us. God's love and mercy guided me to make the right decision, and after twelve hours of flying, Maite and I were at home with my parents. There we both started a new life.

Maite had to learn a new language and a new culture. She had a new family and, more importantly, she began to learn about God and His love.

When Maite was just seven, we learned that her father had been killed in a serious car accident. This news devastated her as she had clung to the hope of one day seeing Dad again.

Since I spent long hours at work and school, my mom cared for Maite. Feeling Maite's emotional pain, Mom suggested to her that she go to her room, get on her knees, and invite God into her life as her Father, Lord, and Savior. Maite remembers Grandma saying to her, "God says in the Psalms:

When my father and my mother forsake me, then the LORD will take care of me.   Psalm 27:10

Maite did what her grandma suggested. When she invited our heavenly Father into her life, He poured all His love into her heart. She received, in a moment's time, an everlasting love from our heavenly Father, becoming instantly Daddy God's daughter.

As I continued to listen to Larry's story, I determined in my heart to pray for his daughter and her four small children and to do whatever else I could to help them. Later, Larry and his wife Barbara came by and shared with me stories of great joy about their grandchildren. Now, I share some of those stories with you in *The Star that Changed a Young Boy's Life.*

Maria Angela Quiñones

1

Grandpa very often looked up at the skies and contemplated them for some time while he was in the field. It was interesting to me to see him with such delight, contentment, and appreciation for something I was not attracted to at all. He spent most of his day in his orchard.

Grandpa loved his farm and taking care of his apple, plum, peach, and quince trees. He knew them very well. He knew when they were thirsty or hungry or when it was time to trim them to make them beautiful and more productive for the next harvest.

I remember having even seen Grandpa talking to his trees. I was very curious about this and tried to hear what he was saying to them. "Grandpa," I said, "are you talking to the trees?"

He laughed and said to me, "Son, they know me. We have spent so much time together that they know when I am worried, sad, happy, or praising the Lord. They know a lot of my stories and dreams. They even know great stories from the past, stories that have never been told because no one seemed to be interested in hearing them."

I didn't understand what Grandpa meant by stories "never told." That sounded very strange to me. So, I said to him, "Grandpa, I would like to know those stories 'never told.'"

"Well, son," he answered, "everything in life has a time, and when it's the right time, I would love to share those stories with you." I could hardly wait.

When harvest time arrived, Grandpa called me and my brothers to help pick the fruit. Some of them were already on the ground, but lots of others were still on the trees. We picked fruit all over his orchard. It was so much fun.

We ate some of the fruits, and I have to say they were de...li...cious! Some went into a basket, and the rest was left for the hungry deer. They, too, loved Grandpa's fruits.

The harvest season was a time of great joy for the whole family. We shared in the work, we ate together, and we laughed a lot while helping Grandpa. Every day I learned more and more about what it meant to be a real farmer.

2

*M*y brother John really loved the quince jelly Grandma made from the fruit of the quince trees. He was constantly asking Grandpa questions such as, "Grandpa, are the quince fruits ready to be picked yet?" and "How much longer do we have to wait for the fruits to be ripe and ready to be picked?"

Grandpa's usual response was, "Remember, son, everything in life—including fruit trees—has a time, a time to grow, a time to develop, a time to be beautiful, a time to produce fruit, and a time for the fruit to ripen and be ready to be picked. We will have to wait a few more weeks."

Having gained our attention, Grandpa went on. "There is something special about these trees. Every year they grow bigger and stronger, and every year their production is greater than the previous year."

Then Grandpa asked us a question: "Do you know what we call that?"

We didn't know, and when none of us answered, Grandpa answered his own question. "We call it grace."

"What is 'grace,' Grandpa?" we asked.

"Oh," he answered, "grace is an undeserved favor from God. It means that we don't deserve it, but God generously gives it to us anyway. We have to be grateful for that."

John was more interested in Grandma's quince jelly. It was a delightful treat, and we all loved it.

I firmly believe that Grandpa's favorite place on the farm was in that orchard. Grandma, on the other hand, cared more about the vegetables we would have on the table. She had loving hands, and everything she touched turned into something beautiful and delicious. Her tomatoes, garlic, squash, onions, and all kind of herbs were the best in the entire community, not to mention her cooking. That made her a queen to us all!

3

*M*y brothers and I all knew that our grandparents loved us a lot, and we also loved them. Our Mom loved us too, and in spite of the long hours she had to spend at work, she always found time to spend with us.

Mom was very good at math, and she made up stories that involved real life problems, situations, reasoning, and calculations and tested us with them. She was very interested in teaching us to think and insisted that we look for at least three options to solving any math problem and then choose the one we thought we might apply with more success. She was never satisfied for us to come up with a simple and plain response to solve any problem. She made us think.

Often we had aunts, uncles, and cousins over, and that was fun. We all loved the tree house Grandpa built for us in the middle of his field. This was our fortress where the dreams of kings, queens, princes, and princesses took place.

From the house to the tree house was a rolling hillside that was our playground. We slid down the hill using a net. That was so much fun. In winter, Grandma created a barrier to stop us from going onto the road. We treasured the time we spent together building fun family memories.

We could not wait to see the snow arrive because we all built snow-men. They were adorned with farmer hats, and they were always holding rakes or any other garden tool we could find in the barn. Everyone in the family, and even friends, were part of our fun winter sculptures.

4

Somehow Grandpa knew the beginning and the end of every season, when it was time for pruning, for feeding trees, for planting new trees, and, of course, for harvesting. He could look at the sky and know that rain was coming, that cold weather would soon overtake us, or that our days would be sunny. Amazingly, he seemed to be able to smell the weather coming. I never knew how he did that, but most of the time he was right.

One day I noticed Grandpa contemplating the sky for a very long time. I asked him, "Is everything okay with the sky, Grandpa? What are you looking for?"

He responded, "Have you ever really looked at the sky, son?"

"Not really," I had to admit!

"You should," Grandpa said, "It speaks to us."

I wondered what he could possibly mean by that? Was he referring to the weather? I knew that the sky didn't really talk, didn't say anything at all, but as I listened to Grandpa, he began to tell me a story about a star that appeared in the east to some "wisemen" more than two thousand years ago. Then Grandpa quoted something from the Bible:

When they saw the star, they rejoiced with exceeding great joy.
                    Matthew 2:10

Wow! That sounded intriguing! "It was a unique star," Grandpa said, "and it shined with a celestial beauty."

I interrupted him and asked, "What is a 'celestial beauty,' Grandpa?"'

"Well," he said, "it is more than what is apparent, more than anyone can see with their natural eyes."

"Can you give me an example?" I asked, still not getting his drift.

"Sure," he responded. He paused for a moment, then said, "Listen, son, celestial means out of the earth and sky, like the sun, the moon, and stars. This star we are talking about shined with a beauty that was not from Earth. This star brought a message from our Creator, God."

I waited, and he went on. "Now we're talking about the heavens. The sky is what we see above us here on the earth, but there is so much more than a pretty blue sky. There are heavens, and those heavens contain stars, moons, and galaxies beyond. It's the magnitude of God;s glory revealed through His creation."

That night I went back to the house with a lot of questions in my mind, but they would have to wait. Mom said it was time for bed.

Our bedrooms were on the second floor. Mine happened to have a big window facing the orchard and part of the sky and heavens. After that conversation with Grandpa, I stood at that window and started looking up, and the more I looked the more I discovered. There was a whole new world that had been there all along, but I had been complete ignorant of it. Grandpa was right. The heavens speak glory, and perfection, God Himself. It took me a long time to finally get to sleep that night.

My interest in discovering the heavens only grew from there until it was transformed into a passion for celestial bodies. The more I read and learned about the firmament above us the more I wanted to discover that new world for myself.

But something was confusing me. As I learned about the stars, the planets, the galaxies, and the universe in general, I kept looking for the bright, shiny star Grandpa had told me about, and I simply couldn't find it.

Winter arrived that year with very cold temperatures and lots of wind and snow. My brothers and I, along with the rest of the family, spent great times together indoors. We all helped Grandma bake. She allowed us to shape our own cookies and add more chocolate or nuts to them as we wished. Her gingerbread and pies and cakes were simply yummy. These were delicious and meaningful memories for my brothers and myself.

Our neighbors could not wait for the apple-blueberry stollen that Grandma generously baked for all of them each year. This was her special treat for all of our dear friends, and they always looked forward to it.

We helped Mom put up the Christmas tree and made a lot of changes to it this particular season. We used family photos, crafts from our Sunday school class, pine cones from the woods nearby, and wooden deer, and we also incorporated new lighting. It looked so very nice!

Christmas was a time of great expectation for us all. We were anticipating lots of presents!

5

Then, one morning, Mom called out, "Wake up, everyone, I found an elf in the kitchen window!"

We all jumped out of bed and ran downstairs. "What? Where?" we were all asking at once.

With a smile on her face, Mom repeated, " I found an elf in the kitchen window!" We thought this was great fun.

Mom said, "I don't remembered having seen an elf in this house before. Did one of you put it there?"

We looked at each other, and then each one answered in turn. "No!" I said.

"No!" John said.

"No!" Lucas said.

Eventually it was agreed that we would put the elf somewhere on the Christmas tree.

The next morning Mom woke us up again and announced, "I found the elf sitting by the front door. Did one of you move it?"

We looked at each other and then responded, "We did not do that, Mom."

"Hmmm, that's interesting," she said, and she grabbed the elf and put it back on the Christmas tree.

The next morning, we didn't wait for Mom to get up and find the elf for us. We got up early and looked for it ourselves. We searched and searched, but without success. When Mom later called us for break-fast, we were expecting her to say as before, "I found the elf," but she didn't say anything.

Eventually we asked, "Mom, have you seen the elf this morning?"

"No," she said, "I haven't seen it this morning. Have you?"

My brother John responded, "We looked for him everywhere but we couldn't find him."

"Well, don't worry about it," Mom said. "Let's finish breakfast and then get your backpacks. It's almost time to leave for school."

As we were preparing to leave the house for school, we saw the elf sitting by our backpacks. John cried out with a loud voice, "Hey, everyone, here's our friend, the elf!" From that day on, we began calling him Body the Elf.

Mom was laughing and saying, "Hurry up! It's time to leave!" She picked up Body the Elf and put him back on the Christmas tree.

While we were on the way to school, John asked Mom, "Why do we find Body the Elf sitting in different places in the house every morning?"

Mom responded, " I think Santa Claus has sent it to check on you boys, if you are doing what you're supposed to at school, at home, and at church—everywhere."

"Everywhere?" asked Lucas, opening his big caramel eyes.

"I think so," Mom said.

"Why?" asked Lucas.

"Well," Mom said "you have written letters to Santa asking him for presents, and Santa Claus wants to know how well you are doing everywhere before he starts delivering presents."

"Oh no!" Lucas responded. "Is that how it works?"

"That's how it works," mom affirmed.

Our youngest brother, David, was not yet ready for school. He stayed at home with Grandma. David didn't pay much attention to these Body the Elf events.

For the next ten days before Christmas we found Body the Elf sitting in different places around the house. Looking for him every morning was great fun.

Two days before Christmas, Grandpa and I went to pick up the mail. To my surprise, there was a letter from Santa Claus addressed to me and my brothers. I could hardly wait for the others to gather around so that I could open it.

When we were all finally together, we opened the envelope, and out came spilling what seemed like hundreds of little colorful and bright stars. What a nice surprise that was! The letter inside said as follows:

Dear family,

My crew and I learned more and more from you, Dustin, and from your family—how well you treat each other, how dedicated you are to your schoolwork and to helping your grandparents around the farm. Your faith has inspired us as well. How faithful you are to God!

I will be coming to your house with your presents. Don't forget my milk and some cookies for me and my helpers!

Santa Claus

Oh my, were we excited!

6

On Christmas Eve, I lay on my bed looking through the window. I thought about the cold but fun day we'd had. I thought about the enthusiasm and joy evident with everyone in the house that day. Everyone had been planning, cleaning, and cooking for the next day.

Personally, I could not wait for the next day to receive all the presents from Santa and from my family. My brothers and I talked a lot about the new toys we would surely get that next morning.

As I was contemplating Christmas Day and what it would bring, I suddenly remembered the shiny star Grandpa had told me about. I jumped out of bed and ran to the window to see if it had maybe appeared again.

I was astonished by the beauty I beheld. The sky, a midnight blue, was full of shiny stars. There was a full moon that lit everything up, and I could even see a tiny part of the Milky Way.

I felt so little compared to the greatness of the vast Universe we lived in. It seemed that I could suddenly see God in all His majesty, power, and love for me. This was more than a fascination for the holy scene I was beholding. I felt reverence, respect, and fear for our great Creator!

As I was contemplating this divine demonstration of God's glory, my eyes were captured by a bright light shining peacefully and quietly in the middle of the night. "This is it!" I said loudly. "This is the star I was looking for." But no one heard me. They were all sound asleep.

I was so totally captivated by the entire view that time and space seemed to stretch out before me, and every single detail of this unprecedented revelation was carved into my heart. I couldn't wait to tell everyone about it the next day.

Since everyone else was already sleeping, I got on my knees alone with God and thanked Him for His amazing creation and for allowing me to appreciate it. I thanked Him for my family, especially my

Grandpa, who always inspired me to do my best in everything.

Then, suddenly, for the first time in my life, I experienced an explosion of joy. I was so happy that tears streamed down my face. I asked God to be my Father and my God. I asked Him to lead me in His ways and to guide me to share His love with everyone I came in contact with.

In that moment I suddenly knew that I was a new creation. Something wonderful had happened to me, and my heart was wrapped with joy and love.

Throughout this experience, I didn't want to so much as blink my eyes, for I didn't want to miss a single thing, and I wanted this special moment to last forever.

Grandpa was right. God's creation speaks of who He is. He is "the

Eternal," "the Great I Am," He who generously blesses all of us with His great love.

When my eyes finally started to close that night, I knew that nothing could ever replace this holy moment in my life, for I had discovered that the God of the Universe loved me and always would. In His peaceful love, I fell asleep that night. Oh, what a Christmas Eve!

7

*T*he moment I woke up the next morning, I ran to Grandpa's bedroom. I wanted to tell him what I had experienced the night before, about my encounter with the heavenly Father and the love that I received from Him, the hope for a new life for my brothers, for Mom, for myself, and for my beloved grandparents.

"Grandpa, Grandpa, wake up," I said. "I've had the best Christmas Eve."

"I'm glad you had it, son," Grandpa said. "Have you seen your presents yet? Are you happy with them?"

"Oh, Grandpa," I answered. "It's not about presents; it is all about love, the love of God. As I was looking at the sky last night, looking for that star you told me about, I discovered that our Creator, God, has created a whole world out of love. Only His divine and perfect touch of love could have made a creation so complete and so beautiful."

"What star, son?" Grandpa asked."

"The bright star you and my Sunday school teachers talked about."

"Oh," he said, "you mean the bright star that led the wisemen to baby Jesus."

"Yes," I said. "I saw it!"

"Well, how do you know it was the same bright star that God sent with a message to the wisemen?"

"I have seen many stars," I told him. "I look for them every night because I'm so fascinated by the heavens and all the celestial bodies. That's how I could tell that the star I saw last night was the same star God sent to the wisemen to announce the birth of Jesus. It looked so different from the rest of the stars. It was exceptionally bright and beautiful."

Sobered and wide awake now, Grandpa looked at me intently and said, "Son, this is the miracle of Christmas! The wisemen were guided by the bright star to see God's Son, Jesus, lying in a manger. He was God Himself, perfect human and perfect God in One. He was born of a virgin and came to this world to pay for your sins and mine."

"The Bible speaks of angels that appeared to shepherds in the field. The shepherds were terrified by the glory of God present in the field that night, but the angels said to them, *'Do not be afraid. I bring you good news of great joy that will be for all people. Today in the town of David a Savior has been born to you. He is Christ the Lord. This will be a sign to you: You will find a baby wrapped in grave clothes and lying in a manger.'"*

"*Suddenly a great company of the heavenly host appeared with the angel, praising God and saying:*

' GLORY TO GOD IN THE HIGHEST, AND ON EARTH PEACE TO MEN ON WHOM HIS FAVOR RESTS!'"

"That's exactly what my Sunday school teachers told us," I said.

"Yes, son," said Grandpa, "but now you know that the love of God for

all of us was manifested on earth through His Son, Jesus. This is more than just a story. You have seen with your own eyes what the wisemen saw and followed. You experienced the glory of God in the heavens last night and, more importantly, you received the love of our heavenly Father."

I wasn't about to interrupt at this point, for I sensed that Grandpa was saying things that were really important to all of us.

He continued, "Christmas is more than a simple exchange of gifts. Christmas is about Jesus, God Himself in human flesh, being present in our world, the Creator of everything. He is the beginning and the end. He is God's perfect love for humanity, He is JESUS, our Lord and Savior!"

"John 3:16 says: *'For God so loved the world that He gave His only Son, that whoever believes in Him [that's Jesus] shall not perish but have eternal life.'*

"Dustin, do you know Jesus' commission?" Grandpa asked.

I wasn't sure what a "commission: was, so I shook my head no,

His commission, "Grandpa answered, "is for us to go and tell everyone about God's love manifested on the cross. There Jesus died in our place, paid for all our sins and the sins of humanity so we can live a life of victory over sin."

I knew in that moment my life had taken on new meaning. God had visited me so that I could tell others about Him. "Oh, Grandpa," I shouted,

Merry Christmas!

Epilogue

As 1 Corinthians 13:8 declares,

LOVE NEVER FAILS!

Jolene's parents demonstrated God's love for her and for her children through their dedication to encourage them, protect them, and pray for them. As a result, God worked on the heart of everyone in the family. Healing took place, salvation came, and the identity of the children was restored. They were now sons of the Most High, Father God.

God wants each of us to know Him personally so we can discover His love for us, His plans and purposes for our life and our true identity—who we are in Christ.

Dear Reader, my prayer for you is that you, too, will discover the God of the Universe, our Creator, and experience the love, joy and freedom found only in Him.

The world makes us to deviate from God's blueprint for our lives. It opens many paths for us to follow with empty promises of happiness ever after. Deceived by the world, we chose to follow it and end up confused and lost from who we really are and what the real purpose of life is. We were not created to fill in the world's blank or to complete a pattern to fit into. We are God's children.

It requires courage to step out of the mold, silence all the voices, including our own, and call upon God. But It is never too late to enjoy and live the life God intended for us to live. The Psalmist declared:

For you formed my inward parts;
you knitted me together in my mother's womb.
I praise you, for I am fearfully and wonderfully made.
Wonderful are your works;
my soul knows it very well.
                    Psalm 139:13-14, ESV

How about you, friend. Do you know Jesus? If not, are you willing to step out in faith and ask God to fulfill His will in you? If you are, please pray with me:

Dear God,

Thank You for showing me that Your love is all I truly need. Nothing in this world can compare to Your unfailing and everlasting love. With all my heart, I believe that Your Son, Jesus Christ, died and rose again just for me.

Forgive me of all my sins, Lord Jesus. Cleanse me and make me new. Renew my spirit, transform my thoughts through Your Word, and restore me completely. Fill me with the joy and hope that only You can give. Guide me to release my past and walk boldly into the new life You have prepared for me.

In the precious name of Your Son, Jesus Christ, I pray. Amen!

www.ingramcontent.com/pod-product-compliance
Lightning Source LLC
Chambersburg PA
CBHW042338040426

42447CB00018B/3479